Determinants of Success

Na'anlep's Persuasive Thinking

First published by Raymond Delmut Na'anlep, 2020
1st impression 2020

978-1-990966-17-0 Print
978-1-990966-18-7 d-PDF
978-1-990966-19-4 ePUB
978-1-990966-20-0 mobi file

Cover design by Sam van Straaten
Layout by Aimèe Armstrong
Set in Sabon LT Std 11/15pt
Printed by Mega Digital

Determinants of Success

Na'anlep's Persuasive Thinking

Raymond Delmut Na'anlep

To my parents who gave me the best upbringing.
To my siblings, all of you believed in my potential.
To my wife, Martina, for your love of cooking that reminds me of home, and your love and commitment to God that reminds me to be a man with integrity and positivity.

Contents

Introduction

Currently, there is a global leadership crisis in many countries and continents, which makes today's world unsafe for everyone. This crisis could be continental, racial, religious, ethnic, gender-based, sectional, and so forth. It is against this backdrop that there is a high demand and a quest for good leadership. That is why this book introduces a new model for producing a new generation of leaders in the world.

Even without a coach or teacher it is possible to become the best role model by looking inwards to extract and harness your innate and raw potential that is lying dormant waiting for discovery and full maximisation. Everyone possesses untapped potential that is awaiting the appropriate time to be unearthed to affect generations of societies. There is always a better you that is yet to be discovered. There are virtues or attributes that you must know about in order to be transformed. This book is intended to emphasise the qualities that matter for you to get to the top of your career, profession or achieve your life pursuits. That is, the essential ingredients necessary for getting you to the top of the social ladder.

What qualities can lead you to the top? It takes a lot of stringent principles and effort for you to be successful and to achieve your life pursuits. There are also character traits that are necessary to put in place during the process of building a successful business, career or any meaningful future endeavour at all levels of life. Life can only be led wisely by adopting great ideologies that can support actions in the right direction which will lead you to achieve a superstar or champion's goals and aspirations. This may never happen in isolation due to potential mistakes that are bound to happen during the course of this journey, which may cause much pain and discouragement, that could challenge the possibility of arriving at a desired destination.

A journey of success does not mean a life that is free from obstacles or other hurdles that have already been experienced by those who have attempted to attain purposeful heights. There is always a beginning and climax of every journey. The same applies to a journey of success. Though it is very wise to prepare and predict the possible obstacles and conditions that may be awaiting you on the way to the top, it may sometimes involve loneliness and separation from society just to discover the secrets to actualise your purpose and destiny.

Determinants of Success provides you with the principles needed to make a good leader. Following the right rules shall produce good world leaders and successful people. Good leadership is in very high demand in the world today. So, raising great leaders is a crucial project for every organisation and for nations of the world. Read and apply the rules in this book to discover, rediscover and sustain every necessary leadership attribute outlined here. Remember, 'readers are leaders' and reading this book will help in transforming you into the desired leader the world needs.

This book emphasises proficient aspects of leadership that have been long neglected but now need urgent attention for a massive change to take place in leadership patterns in the world. Producing good leadership is the best way of solving all impending world problems. Writing about great principles of leadership is the core focus of this book for the purpose of solving the unsolvable world problems. This book attempts to narrow down its scope and focuses on individual attributes, traits and qualities that can help provide the best leaders, but these principles can be applied effectively to leadership styles as well.

This book's attitude is that good people can produce good leadership and that is why discovering great individuals with the best human qualities is the main focus. The book is called Na'anlep's Persuasive Thinking because most of the terms and definitions are based on the author's view, perspective and analytical thinking. This is a wonderful book to change the pattern of world leadership.

Inspiration

Inspiration is the flow of creative thoughts or ideas from the inside that can create a new beginning in the life of a person. It is the conceptual stage of a talent or an idea. I call it the strength or reason behind creative innovations. It is the driving force behind the manifestation of talent.

The result of connecting to inspiration

When you connect to inspiration, it is a morale boost for real performance, discovery and creativity bringing forth new ideas into the world. Inspiration is the raw and unprocessed talent yielding the desired result at the instant it starts to flow. It is the fuel necessary for fulfilling every purpose and destiny. It is also the direction and guide to achieving success in every worthwhile endeavour. Inspiration is necessary for everyone aiming to reach the top of the social ladder in life. If you are inspired, it is always easy to do great things which have no natural interpretation or explanation. Inspired people are great and wonderful people, always active and doing the extraordinary. They are the drivers and captains of various industries in any society. With great inspiration, the world ultimately changes as new innovations and ideas are being produced. Inspired people are mostly brilliant in diverse professions. Inspiration helps leaders to provide solutions to most humans' problems.

Just get inspired to reach the top. Where there are inspirational leaders at the helm of affairs, corruption will be minimised to nothing. Get more leaders with inspiration to keep corruption in check forever. The whole world must launch a more intensive search for leaders with inspiration to see a new face of leadership at all levels. Inspired leaders are able to lead organisations and nations to achieve real breakthroughs. Inspiration makes people, organisations and states far more productive and allows them to strive for greater heights.

The attributes of inspirational leaders

Inspired leaders are made, not born, but there are too few of them in our world today. Inspired leaders are sources of motivation and encouragement, they foster commitment and respect for the culture and values of growth, and steer development and progress in societies. The inspired leaders are those who use a unique combination of strengths to motivate individuals and teams to take on bold missions – and hold them accountable for results. They unlock higher performance through empowerment, not command and control. They inspire others and get real performance. You only need one truly inspiring attribute to lead people and organisations to achieve real success.

The four areas that inspire the traits of leaders and followers are:

1. developing inner resources,
2. connecting with others,
3. setting the tone, and
4. leading the team.

Stress, tolerance, self-regard and optimism help leaders develop inner resources. Vitality, humility and empathy help leaders connect. Openness, unselfishness and responsibility help us set the tone. Vision, focus, servanthood and sponsorship help leaders lead.

It was discovered that people who inspire are incredibly diverse, which underscores the need to find inspirational leaders that are right for motivating your organisation – there is no universal archetype. A corollary of these findings is that anyone can become an inspirational leader by focusing on his or her strength. Although so many different attributes help leaders inspire people, you may need only one of them to double your chances of being an inspirational leader.

Becoming an inspirational leader

Ranking at the top of inspirational leadership traits requires a state of mindfulness that enables leaders to remain calm under stress, empathise, listen deeply and remain patient.

Note also that, your key strength has to match how you create values. Effective leadership isn't generic.

To achieve great performance, you need a leadership profile that reflects the unique context, strategy, culture and behavioural pattern. You have to behave differently if you want your followers to do so. Leaders need to always develop ways of operating optimally. Leaders who inspire people and generate results find ways to constructively disrupt established behaviours to help employees or followers break out of a culture, i.e. weakening routines.

Inspirational leaders recognise the need to select their moments carefully to reinforce a performance culture in a way that can also be inspiring. These are real moments of leadership and truth.

An inspirational leader takes bold actions to change the old ways of doing things by implementing brand new ideas and techniques. They set the tone for the open and honest communications required for a new culture of doing things: 'If you want to change your way of being, you have to change your way of doing'. Leaders can only change by doing things differently. The more often they behave in a new way, the sooner they become a new type of leader – an inspirational leader. Individual inspiration is the gateway to motivational energy for the progress of societies everywhere.

Inspiration is a process that produces leaders with raw talent that may be refined through a higher transformation. Inspiration upgrades, processes and refines people to become the best in the world. This happens through a medium of gradual transformation from a primitive stage to an enlightened stage. What inspiration does is to shape your career, business and future through an insight upgrade.

Inspirational leadership defined

Inspirational leadership is about energising and creating a sense of direction and purpose for employees or followers, including excitement and momentum for change. It involves motivating individuals to strive towards a compelling vision of the future by embracing and embodying values in all aspects of their lives. It includes offering clarity about goals and objectives and ensuring that followers work collaboratively towards a shared purpose. It also includes providing the required resources and motivational support to the people or employees who need to grow and empowering them to be accountable to take responsibility for their own success. It involves progressing from fostering openness and respect in your own leadership style to inspiring those across the organisation or followership to strive towards a new, shared vision for the future or a future state.

Take action!

Inspirational leadership involves taking certain, necessary actions to achieve your goals. A truly inspirational leader:

Promotes individual respect, dignity and integrity at work

- by promoting a culture of respect, fairness and trust where people feel appreciated and valued for their unique contributions;
- by recognising individuals' achievements, knowledge

and capabilities;
- by demonstrating openness to others' ideas or by being influenced by another person (i.e. believing that others have something valuable to say or offer, no matter what position(s) they hold);
- by facilitating open and honest dialogue and creating a safe environment to learn, give and receive feedback; and
- by suggesting possible changes, alternative paths or solutions to others when current solutions or mindsets no longer apply.

Facilitates change and empowers people to grow

- by assigning decision-making authority to others or to those most responsible for the outcome;
- by delegating to others in order to provide them with opportunities for growth, all the while offering guidance, feedback and support to ensure success;
- by encouraging others to reach their full potential by supporting learning efforts that will benefit the self and others, thus creating a culture of continuous learning within the group and throughout the organisation;
- by coaching and developing others by providing timely and constructive feedback and showing sensitivity to diversity and diverse needs;
- by sharing his or her own knowledge and best practices with others for the purpose of assisting in their ongoing development; and
- by promoting understanding of change and effectively managing resistance or negative reactions to change.

Fosters group cohesion, shared purpose and engagement

- by bringing positive energy to the group, communicating a collective purpose and creating a clear line of sight to the value proposition or change agenda;
- by involving others in planning for and implementing change, and, in so doing, gaining their buy-in and helping others deal with their resistance to change;
- by rewarding the contribution of group members, profiling individual and group accomplishments and talents across different functions, as appropriate, thereby engaging people to understand the goals and objectives of the society or of the change; and
- by communicating to societies why change is needed, what the benefits of change are, what is at stake and how the change will positively impact them.

Provides passion for achievement and builds enthusiasm for change

- by generating excitement, enthusiasm and commitment in people by translating the vision, mission and values into terms that are relevant to performance;
- by translating societal change strategies into specific and practical goals;
- by combining clarity of purpose with personal conviction, optimism and a sense of determination to be the best, which results in being viewed as a role model;
- by facilitating society's process of discovery and learning by defining change in a way that they can embrace as their own; and

- by ensuring that others clearly understand and endorse the mission, goals and direction and support them.

Inspires commitment to continued success and ongoing transformation

- by providing leadership to others regarding how to execute strategies that may lead to transition from the current to a future state;
- by taking action to ensure that others understand and endorse strategy and mandate, thereby creating an engaged and energised group to help enable it;
- by being authentic and communicating a long-term vision of change that resounds with others, both within and beyond;
- by genuinely listening to and addressing any resistance or concerns about the future;
- by reinforcing the vision of change and ensuring societal processes and practices are aligned accordingly; and
- by leading and inspiring others to create something truly innovative and distinguishable to gain broad support and commitment.

Why great leaders inspire instead of motivate

Inspiration (not motivation) is the most important leadership trait, fueled by passion and purpose. Here's how top leaders inspire their people.

People often use the terms 'inspire' and 'motivate' interchangeably. Conceptually, they may seem related, but in fact they are worlds apart.

'Inspire' is related to *'in spirit'*. Inspiration comes from within.

The root word of 'motivate' is *'motive'*, which is an external force that causes us to take action.

Motivation *pushes* you to accomplish a task, or work through a difficult event, even when you would rather be doing something else. We are *motivated* by a result.

Inspiration *pulls* you towards something that stirs your heart, mind or spirit. We are *inspired* by a person, an event or a circumstance. An example of a leader that inspires others to accomplish great things is Richard Branson of the Virgin Active group.

When we are inspired, we aren't thinking about the end goal. In fact, when we are filled with inspiration, we want to hold onto that feeling for as long as possible. When we are filled with inspiration, we often don't need external motivation to move forward. The feeling of purpose and meaning is enough to propel us. When we are devoid of inspiration, we must seek out ways to keep ourselves moving forward towards a clearly defined end goal.

Those without a clear vision, mission or purpose often require lots of external motivation to keep moving forward. Those that operate and live from a place of purpose are inspired every day to give 100%. They may get tired, but they can tap into to their higher purpose to be inspired. This is why the most effective leaders are the most inspired leaders, and the most inspirational.

How great leaders inspire

As Simon Sinek taught us in his TED talk, 'How great leaders inspire action', no one follows a leader for the leader. They follow a leader for **themselves**. The most inspirational leaders ignite a spark within their employees and followers that moves them to action. *They don't require motivation to act because they've been inspired.*

How can you inspire your people? What follows is a collection of strategies compiled from various studies and sources.

- **Have a clear vision, mission, and values system.** Inspiring leaders know that the most effective way to enroll followers is to clearly articulate what they believe in, why they exist and where they are going. Followers need something tangible to grasp.
- **Create stretch goals.** Paint a bold picture for your employees and followers that helps them visualise unlimited possibility.
- **Work *with* them.** The most inspiring leaders are highly collaborative. They work alongside their people to make things happen, rather than issuing directives. Two of the most inspiring words are *we* and *together.*
- **Encourage self-development.** Inspiring leaders want their people to develop. They invest in them and they encourage activities that foster physical, intellectual, emotional and spiritual growth and well-being.
- **Acknowledge them.** Everyone seems to have three fundamental needs: to feel safe, to feel like we belong and to feel like we matter. Through acknowledgement and appreciation, we can address all three needs and inspire our people to give us 100%.
- **Invest time in good communication.** Inspiring leaders understand the impact of great communication and the harm of poor communication. They know communication can be a catalyst to growth and use it

as a strategic tool to achieve their goals.

- **Listen.** Again, employees want to know they matter. It's not enough to share your vision. Followers want to contribute their ideas and perspectives as well.
- **Act with integrity; inspire trust.** Employees take their cues from their leaders. They are always watching. To believe in their leaders, they must *believe them.* Inspiring leaders know every action matters.

The next time you want to *motivate* your people, ask yourself how you can *inspire* them. Look *inside* for your answers to drive a devoted following, quantum growth and lasting change.

The good news is that inspirational leadership can be taught, and it can be learned. In fact, all of us possess some of the qualities of inspiring leaders. The secret is to help leaders build upon the strengths they currently have and shore up any qualities that may compromise their ability to inspire.

Bain Inspirational Leadership System

Talent

Talent is a special natural endowment that supports your natural ability to book you a place among great people. It is a high mental ability to acquire a particular skill. Talent does not operate in isolation from personal development and self-enrichment. Talent is the natural gift a person received that is necessary to help encourage leadership. This is an in-born trait that aids your ability, propensity, performance and creativity for doing spectacular things. Talent is the intuition and creativity behind every act of greatness or achievement.

The qualities of talented people

Talent is a driving force for great things and achievements to happen. Talent is a mystery behind discovery, and discovery leads to fulfillment of purpose, while purpose is the seal of success and greatness. Talent can be explosive and life-transforming. Talent always takes people to the top and launches you as a celebrity. It also connects or introduces you to the world of those at the top.

Talented men and women are successful people and great achievers in various endeavours, such as the arts, music, sports, crafts and so on. Talented people always distinguish themselves or stand out among the crowd. They are charming and lovely company to be around. They do things with a difference and in a spectacular manner. Also, in a unique manner which always attracts massive attention from people from different walks of life.

Talented leaders

With well-harnessed talent, an individual can rise from nowhere to somewhere irrespective of their background or limitations. Every talented person is a game changer. Leaders with great talent are imminent personalities with intuition, dynamism, charisma and momentum for transforming organisations with their rare leadership qualities. Such leaders have high possibility of not indulging in common corrupt practices that ravage organisations in various countries on all continents.

With great talent in an organisation, the only vital thing to complain about is training and development. Talent in leadership helps to develop and produce world-class leadership for organisations and nations. The core advice in this book to organisations is to launch a search for employees with talent and then train and develop them for the purpose of maximising their raw potential to achieve organisational goals. It should be a major focus of human resource managers and leaders in the developing world to search for talent and hire such individuals into all hierarchies of government and private sectors.

There is need for a shift from the traditional way of selection and employment to the new technique of searching, selecting and employing more talented employees into organisations and government due to the natural tendency for motivation on the job without supervision or coercion. Talent should be a key criterion and priority for employment as a modern technique for selection and hiring of employees across the board. This factor should also be a yardstick for measuring political appointees.

Due to the high expectation of dramatic change in leadership style politically and managerially, it is a wake-up call to have a pool of talented people occupying strategic positions for the purpose of being dynamic and prompt in responding to the growing needs of the fast-growing enlightened population of the world.

This form of leadership is required and should reflect at all levels of human endeavour. The ability to build leadership on talent development is paramount to all human institutions everywhere in the world. Talented employees are always willing to commit, dedicate and inspire others towards achievement of core organisational goals and objectives. Leaders or employees who are endowed with talents have hidden assets which can be harnessed to make a positive contribution to the growth of any organisation or country.

These leaders can demonstrate vision, focus, stamina, real courage or guts to confront issues, no matter how unpopular it may be. They are unafraid to introducc new techniques to exercise their authority and power. Talented leaders have the credibility and charisma that command attention and compels others top-to-bottom to take you seriously and respect your position.

These leaders don't hold grudges or rub someone's nose in it when they're wrong, instead they focus on what is the best solution and moving forward. In short, real leaders absorb input and take action.

Talented people are naturally endowed, to them popularity is nice, influence is a means, acting honorably is the ideal, and getting things done is the point.

They are the most admirable people to work with who share the spirit and have the skills to turn ideals into solutions. Gifted people can project where they want to go or what goals they want to reach from day one. They know and believe in their abilities, skills, discipline, charisma and determination to change and turn things around. They will only perform better if there is something in it for them.

Transforming your organisation with talent

Leaders or employees with talent are good for challcnging environments and situations where they possess abilities to overcome the common pitfalls of leadership. Generally, people with talent think with vision and get easy answers to upcoming challenges at all times. Sure, most of the creative alignment comes from their minds, which are already offering up a range of ideas to meet every potential human need that could require definite answers or solutions.

Talent attracts extraordinary energy in leaders or

employees in achieving their assigned task and to go beyond that. Great talent helps to enhance the communication skills of leaders and employees in the organisation. It also helps them to develop new patterns and approaches to leadership in a general context.

Everyone with talent is a good team leader, where every team member feels a sense of belonging under his or her leadership. The elements of talent includes consistency, transparency, integrity and authenticity as a professional personality.

Most leaders with talent build internal work relationships, encourage a spirit of teamwork and motivate colleagues to achieve organisational goals or objectives. The talented, engaged leaders and employees make the difference everywhere. Every leader or employee with talent innovates and faces challenges with courage and creativity. They are smart people who lead with intelligence and create an enabling environment, where everyone can be and do their best while still adapting, learning and having fun.

With their vigorous effort, wisdom and vision, they create an atmosphere of enthusiasm, passion and hope among colleagues while driving the organisation forward. Talent in leadership raises both moral and ethical standards to attract respect, honesty, accountability and transparency in the work culture and environment. Talent produces charming, attractive, famous, creative, determined, focused and disciplined people in society.

The choice of placing talented people in leadership positions adds a breath of fresh air to leadership because of skills, fun and general acceptance by the public. For example, the former footballer George Weah is currently the president of Liberia; the Hollywood actor Ronald Reagan became Governor and U.S. President; Jesse Ventura, Governor of the state of Minnesota, U.S.A.; Desmond Elliot of Nigeria was a Nollywood star and is now a serving as a parliament member in the Lagos State House of Assembly; to mention a few.

Talent brings about great followership by others. The application of talent to leadership will naturally change a lot of things, such as to introduce new dynamics into the world of leadership. People with talent in leadership positions attract a wide range of support and loyalty due to the charming nature they possess. Talented leaders or employees always want the big things to happen in order to advance their cause. They always try to put political drivel at bay.

Position them in leadership and get speedy results. Help them find new connections, training and mentorship and you will get better solutions faster to transform an organisation or society.

Talented people are always asking questions with openness, insatiability and curiosity and are never satisfied until they deliver. They utilise their abilities and they recognise that change isn't a threat, so they adapt to it. Most of all, they understand one of the oldest maxims of leadership. Talent is always looking for a way to say yes instead of no. Such leaders listen. They aren't afraid of bad news and criticism, even when it reflects poorly on them. They are open to constructive disagreements and debates, knowing it that it will lead to possible alternatives.

Even when they lose talented people know their voices were heard and the process was fair. That keeps them thinking, inventing and coming forward with new ideas every time. They take ownership of leadership action; they get out to explore, test, discover and interpret. They operate from trust, guide their people towards finding solutions and give their people space to figure out how to solve issues themselves (they are democratic).

They don't betray their followers. When mistakes happen, they back their people up instead of sacrifice them. Through their belief system and support, they give their most effective people permission to do what they do best, make things happen. In return they get their loyalty.

Talented people demonstrate excellence in leadership. That's already established by their character traits and by the example they set. They set standards; the bars are set high and big things are expected every day. They always ask, is this the best we can do? They make sure goals are set to stay focused and to avoid procrastinating. They encourage continuous learning to keep you sharp. They demand results, regardless of precedents, politics, and predicaments.

They don't partake in favouritism, but only merit counts on the basis of performance. Most of all, they recognise limits and human fallibility. They believe in nurturing people and teamwork for maximising the potential to achieve great results.

They are good team players. That is why their leadership will always outperform everyone else's. Leaders with enormous talent often ask questions, such as, "How am I making my people better?". They don't focus on what others say about their followers or employees but look at what they are the best at and what they could do to move things forward; looking, searching or finding the capabilities yet to be realised without faulting anyone.

Talent helps to build confidence and brings forth the potential in a person to deploy into good leadership. Talented people want to be part of something big – an achievement that is remarkable. They want to help create something great and fantastic for the society at large. They recognise great moments and take it seriously. Talented leaders have contagious enthusiasm for motivating others in action that will bring about positive accomplishments. Talent is always looking for positivity and progress. That is commitment. That is passion. That is leadership.

Talented leaders possess the character of fairness in dealing with others. They inspire loyalty, trust and excellence and work to hold themselves responsible to the same rules as those they lead. They don't lead from above or from behind. They lead by example, and they view their people as equals and respect people's opinions while making decisions. They focus on their behaviour before judging others and they weigh up what is important and what is not. That is how they know what is truly fair, and that is how their people know they are being treated fairly too. Talented leaders are consistent in their style of leadership and decision-making. They are reliable, responsible and responsive. They deliver on what they promise. In adversity, they remain composed and focused. They don't point fingers. They gather facts and take action. They understand that everyone takes their cues from them. And they act in the same way they want their people to react.

In the micro world or real world, success is all about talent. Consistency and character are grounded in talent. Such leaders are genuine and successful. They don't carry hidden agendas or say one thing to you and something else to another. And they make themselves approachable and available. They recognise that keeping doors open and confidences in private supply them with a resources that most leaders sorely lack.

Talent is drawn to other talent. And the ability to attract the best people is one of the strategies leaders can use to measure themselves. Great leaders are looking for new talent, who fit with what they need now and where they want to go. So, be the talent needed. Talent goes on the lookout for great potential in societies and in big organisations and the world.

Discipline

Discipline simply means the control measure, or an order, exercised over something. It can refer to mental, moral or physical training. Discipline helps you to break bad habits while self-control helps you not to revisit those habits. Discipline keeps things under full control and gives you a handle over life's circumstances.

Discipline is the quality that distinguishes great people from ordinary people and shifts life to the positive side. Discipline can serve as the control measures put in place to check familiar behaviours or bad habits that can hinder you from living the life of impact or success. It is guidelines and codes of conduct for behaviour while setting out the parameters for actualising the set goals or targets.

Ordinary people do average things while great people do exceptional things. The best qualification for performing exceptional things is discipline. Discipline is necessary to help in goal-setting and the possible achievement of the set targets. This enhances focus that engenders successful ventures. In a real sense, discipline is a self-correctional measure set out to control the ability to derail from the initial intent, vision or plan. Discipline is a tool for personal development or self-training. Well-disciplined individuals have the potential to attain greater heights or success.

Discipline defined

Discipline trains people to act in accordance with rules. It is an activity, exercise or regimen that develops or improves a skill. It is punishment inflicted by way of correction and training. I agree with this definition because discipline allows you to know the rule and regulation that govern a place.

Discipline is defined by the *Oxford English Dictionary* as "a branch of learning or scholarly instruction". Discipline can also refer to the rigour or training initiated by experience, adversity, etc. I agree because it shows you a branch of instruction or learning. It is also a set or system of rules and regulations. Discipline is a positive leadership approach to teach a follower or group self-control and confidence.

As opposed to punishment, discipline techniques focus on what it is we want the individual to learn, and what the person is capable of learning. Discipline is a process, not a single act.

I agree with this definition because discipline is the basis for teaching people how to be in harmony with themselves and get along with other people.

Discipline versus punishment

The ultimate goal of discipline is for people to understand their own behaviour, take initiative and be responsible for their choices, and respect themselves and others. In other words, they will internalise this positive process of thinking and behaving.

Punishment, on the other hand, focuses on misbehaviour and may do little or nothing to help a person behave better in the future. The leader who punishes the follower teaches the follower that the leader, rather than the follower, is responsible for the way the follower behaves. Punishment has negative effects on members of society, such as inducing shame, guilt, anxiety, increased aggression, lack of independence, lack of caring for others and greater problems with leaders or mentors.

Discipline involves training with the aim of producing a specific character or pattern of behaviour, especially training that produces moral or mental improvement. It can also be controlled behaviour resulting from disciplinary training and self-control. Control obtained by enforcing compliance or order. It is a systematic method to obtain obedience. That is a state of order based on submission to rules and authority.

Furthermore, discipline is the basic set of tools we require to solve life's problems. Without discipline, we can solve nothing. With only some discipline we can solve some problems. With total discipline we can solve all problems. Having said that, discipline is needed for the pianist to practice for the concert. Discipline is vital for the student to pass his or her exam. Discipline is mandatory for leaders to achieve their goals and dreams.

How self-discipline will make you a better leader

Leadership styles are learnable qualities that anyone can attain through hard work and self-discipline. While the process of becoming a leader may be simple, it is not easy to do. Everyone can become a great leader, have better self-confidence and achieve success.

Self-control

Self-control has to do with the power of controlling one's external reactions, emotions and so on. It is the ability to keep an individual on track by resisting anything or the temptation to deviate from plans and programmes set at the initial stage for achieving a dream, aspiration or goal. It maintains and sustains very stable steps in the right direction with regard to attaining the place of success in one's life.

The principle of self-control is self-imposed and practised with the ultimate goal of resisting your negative tendencies from affecting the future. Self-control is a moral guide against the quest for perpetrating vices and all kinds of moral decadence. This principle serves as guide, directing your life towards spectacular achievements and success. The principle helps you not to compromise standards no matter the challenges and also guides you to resist any persistent force that can make you fall or become a failure in life.

Discipline and Self-control are strong principles for people of strong character who aim for the top only. People who uphold these principles always get to the top in life.

Self-control in leadership

Many organisations are interested in developing some of their people into future leaders; so they are interested in identifying potential leaders which are those people who show good promise and will be worthy of further investment. Organisations need to identify people who have leadership qualities.

Forgiveness

Forgiveness defined

Forgiveness is the liberating force that sets you free from past offences and mistakes. Forgiveness subdues malice, grudges, pains, depression and stagnation. Forgiveness opens new doors of relationships and opportunities that can also sustain both the new and old opportunities through a process of tolerance, peace and love.

Through the act of forgiveness, you make amends in broken relationships and heal all the wounds of the past. Forgiveness entrenches humility and roots out bitterness from the mind which is the life wire of the human psychology where thoughts are being processed.

Forgiveness and peace

Forgiveness is an esteemed virtue desirable for the general absolute peace of the world. The virtue of forgiveness is increasingly depleting and making the world an uncomfortable arena due to the deplorable peace situation of the world today, including the rising crime rate and negative human developments across the globe.

Love and peace is gradually fading away due to the pronounced absence of forgiveness and the lack of continuous teaching about this key element of human cohesion among societies and the need for its adoption as the ideal means of resolving human conflicts in all dimensions.

Forgiveness is invariably required for solving all human conflicts and needs to be passed on from older generations to younger generations. With this the world could probably enjoy and sustain the required peace and progress for producing better societies which evolve around all the nations of the world. If forgiveness is evident and accepted in human societies, it means peace, love, cohesion and human coexistence is imminent.

Forgiveness as a leadership quality

Forgiveness should be paramount as a lifestyle and a quality for recommendation in attaining leadership positions at all levels of the contemporary society. All leaders at all facets most adopt, preach, and practice forgiveness to achieve a realistic global peace.

Communal peace and harmony are a product of forgiveness. It is a prescribed pattern, philosophy and psychology of life for the achievement of global growth, development and peace. The subject of forgiveness must be taken with utmost seriousness as a world message for peace to be a reality.

The virtue of forgiveness is a great cure to recent violent happenings around the world as it can help to subdue the past pains or grudges and strengthen reconciliations for peace to thrive. No leader is eligible to lead a country to prosperity and fairness with unforgiveness and bitterness.

Focus

Focus is at the centre of our passion or drive. This is the point where vision and determination meet to actualise a dream. It is proof of what exactly you want in life among other alternatives that are competing for your attention and time. It is the focal point of your vision, interest, idea and dream which you are determined to achieve. Focus is the mark to never miss if you really want to get to the top of the social ladder.

Focus and your mindset

A focus on your goals helps to keep some variables in life in check and controls a person's mindset to not miss the mark of destiny. With focus, the tendency to derail in wrong directions or get distracted by other unforeseen occurrences is minimised.

The ability to stay focused is the greatest trait of successful people. Sustain your focus to sustain the future.

Passion

Passion is a strong, barely controllable emotion. It signals intense enthusiasm. This is the impulse, inner drive, intrinsic power or ability that is directed towards a thing or geared towards aspects of a task. Passion facilitates focus with an enormous push to attain the set goal with unusual speed. It is a form of undying love or the quest for an activity or area of interest which, in the long run, will result in a breakthrough or remarkable success in a person's life.

Passion defined

Passion is the inner or silent description of what an individual likes and is ready to achieve or accomplish in life. With passion and a productive mind your vision and goals become possible and attainable. People with passion are great achievers and make it to the top of life's pinnacle, and they tend to remain at the top for long.

Your passion is your interest, your interest is your strength, your strength precedes action and action results in fame.

Motivation

Motivation defined

A motivation is both the intrinsic and extrinsic driving force that leads to accomplishments of tasks and sustainable successes. It is a prompt that stimulates an action, ideas, desire and the direction towards accomplishing a task. Motivation can ignite the drive for satisfaction which is purely born out of the desire for achieving a success. This is a craving, inducement or awareness that can help transform a person's actions into actual achievements.

Every success and achievement are linked to a previous motivation. The act of motivation is the reason, push, desire, craving, predetermination, reaction and action that fast-tracks every human who accomplishes a task. Motivation glows and keeps your hope alive for doing anything viable. It can purposefully make things happen through extraordinary measures.

Motivation is key to success or any worthwhile achievement. It serves as a guide to a leader's actions. If there is motivation, then there is potential for leaders to achieve set goals or targets.

Charisma

Charisma means to be dynamic, benevolent, talented, inspiring and visionary. This is a pragmatic and proactive leadership style. Charismatic leaders are very courageous, determined and articulate to lead others with creativity, intuition, new ideas or innovation. A charismatic leader has ample abilities or potential to change things around him or her for the positive.

A charismatic character

Charisma is a character trait that attracts others to be submissive and loyal followers. A charismatic leader has a formidable personality that can secure the followership of people without reservation. This is a drive or natural tendency of unusual influence that commands others' complete loyalty to a person or leader. It has to do with sustaining the confidence of others, which is also an incredible technique of leadership.

Charismatic individuals are charming in every aspect of life, including personality, leadership style and other important non-verbal gestures. Such a personality is dynamic and flexible to fit into every society.

Charismatic personalities are attractive, charming, elegant, simple, genius, great, humble, friendly and result-oriented in nature. A general belief is that they are magicians at reunification. Get them at the helm of affairs and transformation becomes possible and easier.

An extraordinary leadership quality

Charisma becomes an extraordinary quality for leadership because it is a natural endowment given to those who are capable of providing society with exceptional leadership while the followers remain devoted to him or her. Due to their charming character, it is always difficult to predict these type of people.

A charismatic leader is able to inspire others to gain their support in accomplishing collective and personal goals. What can attract the crowd, spread fame and secure others' attention is the magic of charismatic capabilities. The charming character of these people makes them some of the most successful individuals and leaders in the world. Anytime a country, society or organisation is facing a crisis, the right choice is to enlist a charismatic leader to change the game with their charming and likeable nature.

We need people with this attribute in all hierarchies of leadership. Charismatic leaders have the cure for several types of organisational failures. It could be natural or acquired through administration and self-development.

Determination

This means the firmness of purpose resolved to attaining the set goals; to be resolute at achieving a meaningful target. Determination is the process of deciding, determining or calculating the cost involved in realising a dream. It is the final decision reached in the pursuit of vision.

Determination leads to success

If determination is the watchword, then success and achievement of every goal is possible. People who are determined can never be deterred from or give up on their dreams or life pursuit. It enables you to stay focused and set goals that are properly planned. Determination is the secret for future success and are candidates for greater achievements in your lifetime.

Determined people are successful people and

determination is success in the making. Determination energises success and sustains the vision of a leader during difficulties. Stay determined to get to the top.

Determined leaders don't give up

Determination is a major element of leadership because it can strengthen the ability to stay focused on goals and aspirations. Determined people are persuasive and firm about decisions with set targets as an end result. Individuals and leaders with determination can break barriers. A leader with great determination will not give up on the goals or objectives of the organisation but makes sure it is achievable no matter the cost of implementation.

Determination has to do with the ability to hunt for your dreams, aspirations, goals or set targets and actualise them. This means an unusual bravery towards championing a cause with focus and confidence to achieve set goals or targets.

Determination is a working will to accomplish the purpose or objectives of an assigned or proposed task. Every time a person resolves to do things with determination, excuses are silenced while the voice of confidence prevails and rises against failure by enlisting good leadership.

Determination strategies are what successful people or leaders do to lead a life of impact. It removes fear, doubt, discouragement and mediocrity, and fires up a new strength towards perpetual accomplishments. The ability to succeed in every task is wrapped up inside determination. It is very important for the survival of a leader to succeed at diverse phases of leadership.

Hard work

Hard work involves putting tremendous, tireless effort into achieving or executing a task, while painstaking sacrifices are made. So much of yourself is denied in order to achieve a goal or actualise a definite dream. This quality is identified in those aiming for the top in the pursuit of their goals or greatness. Hard work certainly takes people who apply it with dedication to the top of the social ladder.

Hard work in leadership

Hard work is a rare virtue in leaders who are dynamic, charismatic and determined to attain greater heights of success in the world. It separates successes from failures.

The attribute of hard work is all-encompassing as it includes sacrifice, dedication, commitment, determination, patience, persistence, courage, confidence, hope, faith, focus and unusual diligence in performance of goal-oriented tasks. Hard work requires an excellent spirit to keep you determined and focused on goals and success. It goes hand in hand with rewards, accolades, promotion and success as the end result. Hard work is the topmost secret for success to those who apply it in their daily lives.

Sacrifice

Sacrifice defined

This is the deliberate ability of taking painstaking measures at a particular time targeted at achieving a future success. Sacrifice comes with a lot of determination and focus that could allow you to achieve a positive result later, as predetermined at the planning or forecasting stage. Sacrifice basically means forfeiting the present, temporary pleasures. To sacrifice involves great patience, endurance, resistance, persistence, resilience, commitment, hard work and dedication to the task properly channeled towards future success. There is a great difference between merely starting a task and the ability to stay focused in completing such a task. Sacrifice is the best attribute to facilitate this accomplishment. Sacrifice is a true measurement of commitment to tasks.

Commitment

Commitment involves dedicating yourself to something like a person or a course of action. It is the act of binding yourself intellectually or emotionally to a course or action. It involves devoting more time and strength to accomplishing meaningful tasks or goals.

Commitment is the core and an integral part of achievement. It takes full dedication and attention to an important course of life in order to achieve real success. Without commitment, no meaningful task can be accomplished or is achieved in life.

The committed person

A man that is committed to a task or course and is a man that is successful in life. Commitment also involves focus and a hard decision to pursue a goal to its logical conclusion.

Committed people are great and successful people who can always attain the top of every career or profession in life. Most genius accomplishments come through unwavering commitment to task. Real champions and leaders are products of commitment to a person or assigned task.

With simplicity put in place, your commitment is sealed for achievement.

Dedication

Dedication defined

Dedication is a sort of unusual commitment to an assigned task or the deliberate push to reach a target. It involves full commitment, diligence, loyalty, submission, but above all the undying passion for what you do or believe in. Dedication enhances the result of success. It is an important characteristic to acquire and practise by every leader.

The dedicated leader

This can inspire leaders with outstanding drive to consolidate on achieving some viable set goals. It serves as the preventive measure set against a lazy approach towards goal-oriented tasks. Dedication is key to organisational objectives. The dedication of a leader or person is capable of rekindling the interest and passion towards accomplishing all meaningful tasks. It defines your core desire to achieve set goals or to reach a mark of success. Dedication can spark the unusual desire which will give birth to accomplishments and objectives. Dedication increases the prospect of success and reduces the possibility of failure in the greatest ventures. The dedication of a leader serves as the motivation of the followers. Dedication is a symbol of responsibility to every task or set goal.

Faith

Faith in leadership defined

Faith is a firm belief that precedes an action. Faith receives results in the absence of the proof of possibility. Faith is the conviction that never waits for sight before awareness will pop up. Men and women of faith are rare and quite extraordinary beings in achieving success. People with strong faith are go-getters and successful. Faith mentality is a conqueror lifestyle. Faith is the energy that is directed towards immeasurable success. A man of faith will live so many years ahead of his generation. The eyes of faith never lose focus on its target.

The idea of faith stem from seeing and extracting resources from the invisible world to back up your confidence. Faith energises conviction, courage, affirmation, patience, determination and dedication to productive tasks. Faith can go to an extent of drawing power from the abstract world through a positive mindset and to rightly apply this mindset wherever possible to get the maximum amount success. The strength of faith lies in performing extraordinary things for the purpose of achieving success.

Faith and belief

Faith stems from a firm belief and desire to achieve remarkable results in all endeavours or facets of life. Faith can turn an impossible situation to a possible one in an instant. It can be viewed from different perspectives of religion, psychology or success. Faith can make you a celebrity and astonishing achiever in your generation. Faith provides answers to every difficult life question. Your belief whether it is positive or negative determines your result in life. A firm belief in faith will give results for the world to celebrate because faith is the secret behind so many ideas, innovations or inventions. Faith produces icons in every generation who are creating new solutions to challenging tasks. People and leaders who possess faith are real solution providers. Faith is very strategic in producing leadership that is transparent, accountable, prudent, reliable, trustworthy, steadfast, or steady with allegiance, adherence, commitment and forthright approaches in management of both human and material resources of organisations or countries.

Affirmation

Affirmation refers to your personal view, self-assertions and persistence about a particular concept. It is a state of mind that is positive and convinced about your desires. By making an affirmation it will mean that you take a stand and insist upon seeing your desires come to pass or accomplished as planned. It involves verbalising something repeatedly. Affirmation must be positive so that what you want will happen as planned. Every affirmation should be very concise, brief, simple and to the point. It is important to continue saying it and keep doing it until is successful.

Affirmation in leadership defined

Leaders need to cultivate such an attitude for the purpose of accomplishing difficult task. Affirmation helps in surmounting problems at various stages of life. It helps individuals to create wealth, true love for people and helps improve the well-being of their life. This leadership trait strengthens faith, hope and fulfillment. Affirmation is a trademark for great leaders. Get affirmative about every one of your desires, anticipations or future goals. Every affirmation must come from a very strong belief or faith in the ideal things.

Courage

Courage in leadership defined

The concept of courage entails facing the fiercest situations of life. Courage is a confidence build-up that is beyond the boundary of fear. The presence of courage easily extinguishes fear. Courage cannot be well defined in the absence of faith and the two terms are synonymous that can't be separated.

Faith serves as a platform for courage, while courage supplies faith with the ability to perform triumphantly. Courage remains the mask that can unravel faith correctly. Courage comes from a relaxed mind with full concentration. Stability of the mind is a main factor to build courage. The total courage of a person is equal to success while the total cowardice is equal to total failure. Courage produces the determination for success and the ability to overcome possible obstacles.

Our courage is the bliss of hope while hope is a drive to success. Every potential successful person needs a great measure of courage to dissipate any rising pessimism. Courage is the enduring ability to sustain goals and aspirations even amid messy situations that represents danger and discouragement. It is the attribute of heroes. The measure of courage of individuals can transform everything in the world and make things happen beyond the ordinary.

The importance of courage in leadership

The best and most charismatic leaders have courageous personalities. Every leader aiming to perform actions that will change lives, organisations and societies must possess heroic courage for the execution thereof. To achieve success and provide good leadership we need to develop a heroic mind, disposition or spirit. The exercise of courage has to come from the heart, inner strength or innermost feelings whereby it also culminates in dauntlessness or bravado. The attribute of courage enables a conviction and belief that produces valour, intrepid boldness and fearlessness in confronting all kinds of dangers while making critical decisions. The ability to do the most difficult or scary things demands a whole lot of courage by courageous personalities. It is a basic tendency to conquer our fear in the most dangerous situations. Courage means the exchange of the unbelievable with optimism that is capable of changing the unfavourable to the favourable. It means to be brave and confident and to do what you believe in.

The character trait, courage, entails the ability to provide a strong control and willingness to deal with difficult and unpleasant circumstances. Courage is our inner ability to assemble and produce quality mindsets to combat or confront uncertainty, intimidation, or difficulty with bravery. We can say courage facilitates a morale, desire and ability to act rightly in the face of discouragement or opposing situations. Courage involves discipline, perseverance, patience and classical virtue of fortitude. It is also right to say, courage is the most esteemed human quality because it guarantees the existence of other qualities. Courage is what enhances the consistency of other human virtues.

Our courage is what counts at every point of human development. We think and act for ourselves by possessing real courage to start all over again. The act of courage is necessary because it touches on everything about life and success. And the most vital thing is the courage to follow your heart and intuition while solving lifelong problems or making decisions for the future. Everything we desire for a good life is found and secured in courage alone. While everything is possible with the right moral courage.

Hope

Hope defined

Hope is the life given to the future irrespective of fear or doubt. Hope speaks well about the future in the midst of dwindling circumstances. The power of hope can fire out doubt and destroy the grip of failure on destinies. Hope anchors the future while the future anchors success. Hope emanates from optimism which is a product of a positive mindset. Hope is a pattern of positive thinking that facilitates confidence, courage, and optimism this in turn leads to the achievement of your goals and aspirations. Hope removes the barrier of mediocrity and despair while it strengthens the psychological capacity to rise above discouragement.

Hope in leadership

Hopeful leaders have the ability to transform a society or organisation. There is a need for a leader to be hopeful in order to be able to project future growth and development so that they can secure a desired future. Hope puts optimism on track which will lead to achievements. Hope is necessary for the purpose of building a strong expectation while planning and executing the objectives of an organisations or society. The build-up of a desire and expectation via hope helps to easily carry out every task and get things done within the stipulated time frame.

Hope supports the survival of our inspirations because it backs up inspiration with expectations, this refers to the feeling of confidence, trust, and enthusiasm. The joy of leadership can only be maximised through the hope and anticipation of great happenings of a positive nature. A visionary leader can achieve more goals through hope. Thinking with a sense of hope will help to envision and generate the assurance or possibility of achieving the most of our goals in life. Hope gives us the expectation that what you long for is going to happen.

The character trait of hopefulness helps everyone to develop an attitude of anticipation for the future. This means that a leader has an expectation of fulfillment and success. Such exceptional virtues help leaders to remain hopeful and desire something positive to happen. It is a feeling of optimism about life's general issues.

Every leader needs hope as a leadership trait. Hope as the best state of mind is necessary for people at all levels of leadership. Hope motives people to take proactive steps to adopt positive changes and enhances a quality lifestyle.

Above all, hopefulness helps in maintaining a positive drive in the pursuit of a particular goal or set of goals. Hopeful thinking strengthens an individual's determination to achieve their personal or organisational goals despite possible challenges.

Hope remains the best therapy for the passionate and enthusiastic attainment of goals by maintaining personal motivation and a greater sense of optimism. This means that hope is an important concept for producing role models in leadership. Hopeful individuals are potential future leaders. Equally hope means a sunrise putting a smile on the face of success.

Conviction

The foundation for the survival of hope is conviction. Rather Mr. Conviction is the personal assistant to Mr. Hope in the world of social economy. The former is the host, while the latter is the guest. Add the two together and the world will greatly celebrate your remarkable success. The entire process of success demands conviction to fire up your courage.

Conviction defined

Conviction is the backup and support that can sustain an unbeatable courage. Conviction creates a power to produce hope which will make most of our goals achievable. A good leader needs to possess a high level of conviction to achieve both personal and organisational goals. Conviction is necessary in the pursuit of goals and relevant in charting a new path to success and diverse accomplishment in life. We need our conviction to build courage which can sustain our future and fortunes. Conviction helps raise hope while hope sustains the focus on goals and objectives by giving it a specific direction and achieving all set targets.

Our conviction enables hope and faith for us to stay focused on projects and programs of success and purpose. The ideas, innovations and inventions that rule the world are products of people with conviction. Conviction works with faith, hope and courage to make great ideologies possible in solving societal problems. Conviction enhances strong beliefs, opinions, views, thoughts, attitudes, positions and ideas to make difficult situations in society change into positive ones.

The importance of conviction in leadership

Leaders with the virtue of conviction never fail in executing their task. These leaders do what they believe in and stand for always. Leaders with conviction are optimistic and courageous in transforming their society. Any opinion held on the ground of conviction is unshakable and need no further proof or evidence. Conviction is a positive element of positive change. Conviction strengthens assurance, certainty, confidence and satisfaction which help to sustain focus on your goals and objectives. With conviction everything becomes so real and true to help you achieve effective and efficient results. Conviction provides proof or evidence to support visions that can change the future. It is a product of a positive mindset. This is the only strong belief or feeling which enables people and leaders to make the right decisions and implement such decisions. Conviction is necessary to dislodge fear and doubt by restoring confidence while moving forward to take actions towards progress or success. Conviction is a positive law of success. Every decision reached with conviction is unshakable, strong and positive.

Endurance

This is the ability to strike a balance between trying moments and successful moments that lie ahead. It is the point between the difficult times and the possible, fulfilling times of your life. Endurance sustains a person in order to remain stable and stay focused even in difficult times in their life. Endurance is driven by the power of hope.

Endurance defined

Endurance is one of the key secrets of great and successful people. People who usually endure difficult times will live to see better days in their life. Endurance helps to safeguard the future for those who make it a lifestyle. With endurance, one can never miss the mark of greatness. Successful people adopt it as a means of transformation until they get to the final destination in life. People who endure don't give up even when the challenges are fierce. Only those who have the ability to see the future can endure the difficult present situation.

Endurance is a trait of greatness because the lazy and mediocre cannot make endurance a lifestyle. It is very important to possess a mentality that should be able to endure and ignore the wild forces of resistance stopping us from reaching our goals. Endurance is an attitude that helps successful people break barriers of desperation through discipline. An illustration of endurance is an athlete that wins a race not because they are first to start the race but first to reach the finish line in a marathon.

The importance of endurance in leadership

Endurance enables patience and sustainability which leads to successful accomplishments in business or leadership. Any student ready for excellence must endure the processes of reading, writing and passing all examinations to receive their final certificate of graduation with flying colours. It is the same virtue that a leader needs to succeed. Endurance is the right attitude and approach to succeed as a leader because it aids you to focus on your goals and not the challenges. An enduring spirit is a beneficial attribute for the actualization of predetermined objectives. Endurance goes beyond saying, to do what is necessary to get the end result.

Endurance means to be strong mentally to champion a cause and achieve results to the maximum. Enduring leaders set goals and accomplish them. Leaders with endurance break barriers by taking one step at a time.

Endurance has a lot to do with the mindset of a person. Every accomplished task begins with your mind. If you don't envision yourself doing it first, you will never do it at all. Endurance makes impossibility seem like a thing of the past while giving power to your now so as to progress up to final accomplishment.

Patience

Patience defined

This is a rare virtue among ordinary people. It is the ability to ignore the circumstances in life that can deter someone from success. Patience is the resolute position to wait for the expected positive change.

Patient people don't accept defeat easily but persist until a positive result is achieved. Patience is a decision not to react to any discouraging and unfriendly situation. Patient people withstanding all forms of maltreatment by others on the way up or to success.

Patience is the key ingredient for success

Without patience, it is not possible to climb the ladder of success. Patient people even live longer and that will extend their success too. Patience is a necessary ingredient for anybody who wants to make it to the top of the social ladder. Patient people are successful people in life. If you are out for real success, then patience is a compulsory attribute to adopt and also a necessary lifestyle for every successful individual.

Persistence

Persistence defined

Persistence simply means to maintain and stand no matter the adversity. Persistence is to stay focused and to remain stable even in the midst of discouraging circumstances. Persistence helps to give success a push in times of resistance. Persistence conquers resistance on the path to success.

This is the only attribute that can destroy and uproot fear, difficult and discouraging situations in order to pave the way for success to prevail over failure. It subdues negative tendencies that can hinder success. Persistence is the oil that adds strength to success. Persistence can see through the eyes of possibility even in an impossible situation. It has the utmost strength to prevail over negativity. Persistence is a recommended key for success and greatness. This is the power that sustains hope while hope is the fuel of success.

Humility

Humility defined

The trait of humility has no substitute when it comes to the issue of success. It means bringing yourself down even when you are the most superior among others. The ability to serve others even when they are supposed to serve you. Humility is the opposite of pride. It is the only strong character trait that can say no to pride and go ahead to adapt to a simple lifestyle. A humble person will never say, I am too big to serve others who in turn can also bless me for greatness. Humility never undermines other people.

Humble people accept simplicity as a secret for success. Achieving success and greatness is very easy if humility is a lifestyle. Humility indicates greatness through the display of exceptional character traits. It can always be mistaken for foolishness but if properly applied it will meet the target in the long run. Humility is one of the mysteries of success that ordinary people find difficult to adopt as a key for success, rather they despise it.

The importance of a humble leader

Humble people are charming people to be with and enjoyable company to live or work with. Humble people are the best managers of big business or firms. They perform lots of magical things with their rare and exceptional attributes to expand any business or organisation that they manage. This means acknowledging the relevance of others helping you achieve your dreams and aspirations without despising your subordinates in the organisation. Humility represents simplicity with the awareness of individual self-esteem but wisely avoiding empty ego or pride. For organisations, societies and countries of the world to prosper there must be a deliberate effort to discover humble personalities and place them strategically at the helm.

Submission

Submission is the collective loyalty to a superior, an overseeing authority or constituted authority in a particular set up. Submission brokers a harmonious work relationship among superior and subordinates in a workplace, organisation or any group. It is a necessary ingredient for climbing the success ladder.

Submission in superior-subordinate relationships

Submission is the lubricant that greases a superior and subordinate relationship while the relationship paves the way for a successful career. Subordinates who submit to their respective superiors are always on the list to occupy the best place in organisations. The act of submission places you where your contemporaries cannot. Willingness to duly submit is a plus for any kind of success.

Submission is one of the mandatory keys of success. It is not optional, it is rather a must for people who aim at making it big in life. Submission can easily turn things in your favour irrespective of stiff opposition from other quotas. Submissive people always have the best place in the heart for their managers or those in authority when it comes to a promotion. Submission is really a secret code for greatness in life.

Loyalty

Loyalty defined

The term loyalty refers to a complete 'yes' action or answer to what you are commanded to do by the highest or immediate authority in a given place. Loyalty is a symbol of agreement to terms and conditions of operations and superiority. It is a license for winning the mind of every superior without being subjected to further demands.

Loyal superior-subordinate relationships

Loyalty helps build a healthy relationship between superior and subordinate. It is the display of outright submission in alliance to your superior's actions. The act of loyalty does not need any perfect infallibility on the side of the superior. The subordinate accepts the superior as is without saying 'but' before submitting to the superior.

Loyal people are few and are the most qualified for top positions. It is an attitude of great people because of the high level of understanding and patience that they can exercise in negative situations. Loyalty is the opposite of disobedience. It does not look at the weakness of the superior before resolving to obey the instructions. Loyalty is a strong attribute of leadership.

Obedience

Obedience defined

The act of obedience refers to total loyalty or submission to your elders, rules and regulations or constituted authorities in society. Obedience is a trait that anyone that makes it a lifestyle to excel in life with less stress has. It is an enviable and eminent character trait for those aiming at attaining different heights in leadership and success. Natural laws and human laws are meant to be observed and obeyed but any attempt to break existing laws or protocols will always incur hazardous consequences. For every action there is an equal but opposite action. In essence, when we exhibit a negative force in thought, word, or action, that negative energy will come back to us. The result of every act of simple obedience is always positive and rewarding while the act of every disobedience is always negative.

Obedience within leadership

The attribute of obedience is a mandatory leadership requirement and a sign of good followership. This is the only way to face out autocracy, dictatorship and totalitarian leaders from communities and governance. There is a need for leaders who can obey the rules and for followers who are obedient to constituted authorities for us to better our societies.

Wisdom

Wisdom defined

The attribute of wisdom means that you possess good judgment based on a wealth of experience. Wisdom is having wise plans and making wise decisions. Wisdom is the act or ability to do exceptional things. Wisdom means to be wise beyond your years. Wisdom is called 'the eyes of awareness' – a trait not possessed by everyone. Wisdom is the intuition and enablement that pave way for greatness. The presence of wisdom is accompanied by outstanding results to which others cannot measure up. It is not an attribute for mere people.

Wisdom sets the pace to make a difference in your world. Wisdom supplies us with the answers to unexplainable and difficult situations. It separates the ordinary people from the extraordinary people. When you achieve wisdom, you will be announced to the world as a celebrity. Men and women of wisdom are outstanding people with remarkable records. Wisdom produces people who create historic events. People with wisdom are rare in society but where they are present, the top is always reserved for them. If you possess wisdom, it places you in a better position to achieve greatness in all spheres of life.

Wisdom and success

Wisdom is the opposite of folly. Wisdom can take people from the bottom to the top in an unusual way. Wisdom produces a high degree of prudence and wise judgment in in every situation in life. It is also accompanied by a high level of discernment when it comes to matter of handling difficult situations in general. So, wisdom is a virtue and a qualification for success and a place at the top of society or organisation. Wisdom also means the wise application of our human endeavour.

The attribute of wisdom stands alongside all forms of respect for rules and order for institutions and diverse communities in order to run optimally.

Leadership and wisdom

Through wisdom, history records that king Solomon remained the greatest leader of all times in the history of human existence. Therefore, wisdom is a rare virtue of leadership and leaders must desire to possess wisdom as an attribute. wisdom is a necessity for good leadership and the making of good leaders at all realms of human existence.

Understanding

Understanding defined

This means to have an intelligent or foreknowledge of an event, person or thing. Understanding is a comprehensive awareness about anything that needs an interpretation and interpretation of a given phenomenon. That is an exhaustive finding that give the right insight about an event, people, things or a general concept.

Through the demonstration of a high degree of understanding people in history made a unique impact in the world in their areas of discipline leading to great reforms and transformation. People who understand are solution providers in every difficult situation. Understanding distinguishes professionals from lay-men. Understanding conquers ignorance and sets the way for creativity, achievements and a successful lifestyle. Understanding illuminates the mind which translates to enlightenment in all ramifications. Understanding is the only compass that gives us the right direction in life, even when others are going astray. It can single a person out of the crowd in terms of decision making and standing in life. It paves the way for performance with a promotion as the end result. Understanding brings about excellence and distinction in your career and all other activities that can place you in a class with great achievers.

People with understanding possess a potential for outstanding success. These types of people attract change in organisations and societies. Automatically, it means that understanding is a necessary ingredient to have a place at the top of the social ladder, to be successful and to attain all levels of greatness in your life.

Transformation

Transformation in this context is a gradual and positive personal growth and development. The concept also applies to the transformational process of a society, association, community or country. Transformation is relevant for progress and prosperity as it concerns the future. Transformation can enhance positive change in individuals and societies. This is the process of change, modification and conversion of anything in a similar manner. It is all about giving something a new look, form, nature or appearance to become better. It equally means to supplement or replace the old with something brand new.

Transformation in leadership

Every leader strives for personal and organisational change to remodel themselves or the organisation. This is the mark of a significant change in the life of a person, leader or organisation. Transformation is an enviable process to adopt by a leader to help in achieving personal and organisationally set goals. The conceptualisation of transformation requires a lot of efforts in positive thinking, planning and forecasting of the future. With transformational processes in place every achievement will become possible and on target. It makes excellence the quest and desire of great people.

Integrity

Integrity defined

This refers to the integrity of your brand, trademark, principles or legacies. It refers to those attributes that you make use of to define your personality and the way you conduct yourself in public while trying to do routine business in order to achieve your set targets. Integrity is a basic trait to facilitate your success. The absence of integrity can challenge the ability to sustain your success to be able to last a lifetime. Every act of integrity pays in the long run. Integrity is a marker for all potential leaders who anticipate success in the future. The ability to possess integrity is a straight path to attain great heights and to settle you in a strategic societal position.

Integrity in leadership

Integrity is what makes you the most suitable leader for the most lucrative and reputable positions in any organisation. This trait in leadership has been very rare among contemporary world leaders therefore leaving so many organisations with a dire need. Up and coming leaders are encouraged to cultivate this attribute as they prepare to climb the ladder of the social strata in the world.

Vision

Vision is the picture of the unseen that forms the reality of the future in our material world. Vision gives momentum to focus and focus is the guide for passion and the end result is meaningful success. Vision is a necessity for every candidate of greatness and success. It is the ultimate direction for maximising potential and fulfilling destiny. Vision keeps people focused on every goal, objective and target set ahead to attain remarkable success. It is the quiet voice behind the pursuit of goals and objectives.

Visionary people

Visionary people are successful people in every human endeavour. Vision means to be stable, focused, determined, and undeterred in every life pursuit. Vision is a key that unlocks all future possibilities through a firm decision that is backed up by total awareness about the final outcome. Profitable and productive ventures are by-products of a vision. Vision conquers all the barriers of failure through the foreknowledge of the promising future which lies ahead. It clears every doubt and fear about the future due to the initial level of certainty you have about the future. Vision has the ability to magnify our ambition and get our desired future. Vision conquers mediocrity and fear for the unknown. Visionary people are extraordinary achievers in every field of human endeavour. These are people found in the same class as those that give birth to great ideas, innovations, skills, talents and inventions in the areas of music, arts, sports, leadership, sciences and technology.

Vision and success

Vision is a necessary ingredient to attain greatness and parallel success in life. Vision is the encyclopedia for success at an immeasurable level. Vision is the act of seeing, an idea vividly in the imagination. Vision allows us to see things from afar through imagination and begin to project, forecast and plan the execution of such a vision immediately. Seeing the unseen and conceptualising it into reality will give birth to tremendous success. Vision always refuses and resists discouragement because of the strong sight involved. The sense of direction is purely captivating. Visionary men and women are great icons and destined for the top. There will be no positive change if there is no vision, but a clear vision is what can sustain an enduring change at all levels of societies. Leaders need to be visionaries to be able to lead well.

Self-esteem

Self-esteem defined

Self-esteem refers to self-discovery, conviction, ego, image, self-awareness which assists to keep a person or leader focused and enthusiastic. It is about what you know about your worth, value and capabilities which help to stimulate courage, confidence and positive perspective about yourself. This helps boost the desire to attain great and noble heights through a successful lifestyle. Self-esteem is a basic element of leadership that keeps a leader motivated. This quality can silence the thundering voice of discouragement from holding a leader down with despair.

Leadership and self-esteem

Self-esteem attracts unequalled respect from followers and

the society at large. There is no room for excuses when you are building great self-esteem. It is a trait that puts you in the same class as world leaders. This quality gives you an uncontestable position in every sphere of life. The journey of success becomes smooth and pleasant if your self-esteem is positive. Self-esteem boosts your confidence and protects you from other people not flattering you to the point of discouragement and it will keep any anticipated disappointment in proper check. It's about being in love with yourself and cherishing everything about yourself. Please note, that self-esteem is different from arrogance or pride. This is a positive evaluation of your self-worth for the purpose of success. You can call it thc lifestyle of champions.

Kindness

Kindness and leadership

The virtue of kindness is what makes a leader respond to the need of the masses and to be able to feel what the yearning of the general public is. Kindness produces a benevolent leader who is responsible and responsive to the welfare of others in an organisation or community. The attribute of kindnesses makes a leader loving and caring to the needy and proactive in helping or solving societal problems. It bridges the gap between the leader and the followers where all channels of communication are open for finding solutions to the collective needs of everyone.

Kindness is a seed that anyone can sow and in the future they will reap accolades and respect. Behind every kind deed is a charitable spirit. With this gesture a leader can fairly distribute resource without sentiment or bias and by doing this build a society free from division or discrimination. Kindness is a solid bridge between a leader and the public which aids in linking a leader's intention with the physical development plan.

This particular attribute of leadership is very rare, but it is in high demand in our present precarious generation. It is lacking in the contemporary class of leadership we have today in the world at the same time is a major deficiency among our ordinary masses or lower-class people. Kindness is a virtue that can solve a lot of world problems, ranging from social perversity, immorality, vices, terrorism, racial and ethnic discrimination, religious diversity and prevalent corruption among world leaders. The message of kindness is a great cure to the ideology of selfishness or egocentrism among today's ruling class or world political dynasties.

Lifestyle

Lifestyle defined

A lifestyle is an individual view, approach, dimension and general outlook towards the core values of life. Your lifestyle will define the course of your life and determine the possible steps that may be involved in taking critical decisions about life's general issues. This is the outward expression of a person's inner choice and mental disposition about the world. It goes a long way to affect the process of decision-making and the final application of every decision made concerning your personal worth, values and accomplishments. The lifestyle of every person is the real definition of their entire personality.

A lifestyle could influence the choice we make in terms of decisions regarding matters that are of great relevance to becoming the best personality or influential leaders in your generation. A positive lifestyle will produce a positive personality while a negative lifestyle will produce a negative personality. Negative lifestyle is the enemy of success while a positive lifestyle is the power behind every greatness and success. Nothing disqualifies and stands against the growth, progress or success of a man such as a negative lifestyle. Your lifestyle is the key to your success in life.

A lifestyle of leadership

Lifestyle is key to goal-setting and the procedures on how to actualise your visions, dreams and aspirations at the appropriate time by applying the right approaches in implementing all of them. A lifestyle can be attractive or disgusting, repelling other people who could serve as important vehicles in accomplishing success. A lifestyle is very instrumental to the development of an individual's life and success. Proper precautions are necessary to check our conduct in public and to avoid poor image and indecency that can hinder success and a quality leadership style as it relates to general public relations.

You (Personality)

Personality defined

This refers to an individual's personality, attitude, qualities, limits and I.Q. (Intelligence Quotient). This can serve as a possibility or serve as the barrier to success. You can make or mar your future. You are the gateway to everything that can affect your entire being or existence. You can be a blessing or a curse to your progress and success in life.

Leadership and the 'you' factor

The 'you' factor is a great determinant of a successful lifestyle. This determinant is very critical in making it to the top in life. Even if all the other factors mentioned in this book are working for you in absence of the 'you' factor, there is a likelihood that everything will fall apart and work against your success. In the attempt to work towards greatness and success in life, the issues of self (i.e. the you factor) must be address properly.

The personality of a person is the key to opening every door of success closed against such them. It is said that, "Personality opens doors and character sustains it".

Nothing hinders career progress or growth such as the individual's personality and nothing opens doors of opportunity for career progression or growth such as personality which is the 'you' factor. Good behaviour attracts good recommendations, and bad behavior attracts negative recommendations.

The only self-motivating criterion for promotion is your outstanding personality. The paramount criterion for measuring people to qualify for the next level or position is the 'you' determinant. All the other determinants mentioned in this book are embedded in it and also depending on it for their survival and impact!

Books, articles & references

John H. Zenger (2009) The Inspiring Leader Unlocking The Secrets Of How Extraordinary Leaders Motivate.

Wayne Dyer (2017) One Leadership.

Richard Bronson (2017) How To Make Business Decisions.

Andy Stanley (2019) Seven Keys To Effectively Manage Conflict.

Eric Garton (2017) Inspire; How To Be An Inspirational Leader.

Ram Charan (2017) The Potential Leader.

Leading Blog (2017) The 9 Behaviours Of Great Leaders.

Pastor Rick Warren (2017) 6 Vows Great Leaders Are Willing To Make And Keep.

Hardy, Benjamin (2018) Willpower Doesn't Work.

Duhigg, Charles (2012) Power Of Habit.

Clear, James (2018) Atomic Habits.

Gordon Leider (2017) Were The Founding Fathers; Great Leaders.

Leading Blog (2017) Ego Free Leadership.

Tian Moulman and Eric Barton (2018): Why Inspirational Leadership Alone Is Not Enough.

National Council Canada Modified (2019) Behavioural Competence.

John Adair (2009) The Inspirational Leader ; How To Motivate, Encourage And Achieve Success.

Jeff Schmitt (2013) 12 Ways To Be The Leader Everyone Wants To Work For.

Upcoming Title

Paradigm Shift
(Mental Revolution)

Introduction

This is a pattern or mannequin model of intellectual revolution and transformation which must serve as the bedrock for every significant development and productiveness via every country focused on a stable future at all spheres of its country wide of life. It could be for the cause of changing lives, transforming Nations and intellectual ability of a human resource of countries at a number of levels and phases of growth and development. Nothing can stop a country or a man with the right intellectual mind-set from accomplishing a desire, targets, goals and objectives, and nothing on earth can help a country or a man with the wrong intellectual mind-set or disposition to achieve greatness.

Every generation of people, country or continent needs an innovative, revolutionary and transformational shift in mental potential to impact the needed heights it desired. There is dire need for mental revolution and transformation, a radical shift in the way we see the world around us and do things is necessary. This will equip us seriously change the lives of people, nations and continents, to create symbolic and symbiotic value chain for upcoming generations.

The human thought stays the most potential vehicle to drive significant growth and development. The mindset is the seat of wisdom, ideas and factory of greatness. Every change most commence from within and to reflect on the outside. The human mind is unlimited in nature.

Raymond Delmut Na'anlep